PSALTER of LECTIO

Building a Personal Psalter in the Ancient Practice of *Lectio Divina*

Basic INTRODUCTION to PRAYER

Introduction	4
Psalter? Lectio?	5
What is *Lectio Divina*?	7
Lectio Continua	9
A Pray-er's Partial Bibliography	11
Scripture Used in this Prayer Experiment	12
Psalter Comparison	14

VIGILS, LAUDS, MIDDAY, & VESPERS for each day:

SUNDAY	16
MONDAY	28
TUESDAY	40
WEDNESDAY	52
THURSDAY	64
FRIDAY	76
SATURDAY	88
Aware Prayer	100
Night Prayer	101
Index of Psalms	106
A Reading Plan for *Lectio Continua*	107

Compiled by Stephen Joseph Wolf, former priest & spiritual director

Psalter of Lectio, revised
**Building a Personal Psalter in the
Ancient Practice of** *Lectio Divina*
Copyright © 2012, 2023
Stephen Joseph Wolf
All rights reserved. No part of this publication may be reproduced in any form, except for the inclusion of brief quotations in a review, without permission in writing from the author or publisher.

Opening and closing prayers are from *The Liturgy of the Hours (Four Volumes)*
© 1974, International Committee on Enlish in the Liturgy, Inc. (ICEL).
All Rights Reserved.

The Antiphon for Night Prayer is as sung at the Abbey of Gethsemani.

Scripture used in this book is by Stephen Joseph Wolf, following
his meditation rendering in *Rainbow Psalms in 30 Days.* Sources include
The Interlinear NIV Hebrew-English Old Testament by John R. Kohlenberger III
(Copyright 1979, 1980, 1982, 1985, 1987 by the Zondervan Corporaton), and
the Interlinear Translation by Alfred Marshall in *The NRSV-NIV Parallel New
Testament in Greek and English* (Copyright 1990 by the Zondervan Corporation).

Spiritual Adoption (page 35) appeared previously in *Gospel of Life Prayer Cycle.*
The *Spirit* prayer (page 100) is adapted from a song by Serafina di Giacomo.
The seasonal mid-day Prayers for Vocations are by Stephen Joseph Wolf
with gratitude to St. Stephen Catholic Community.
The cover photograph is from St. Thomas Aquinas School in Thomassique, Haiti,
sister parish of St. Henry Church in Nashville.

ISBN 978-1-937081-01-0

printed and distributed by Ingram Books
published by **IDJC Press**
www.idjc.org

Dedicated to
grandmothers and great-grandmothers
who were a blessing to my youth
all gone to heaven:

Loretto Quest Wolf,
Rosemary Watson (Tody) Gregory,
Rachel Davis Watson, and
Matilda Turner Gregory,

three Catholics and a Southern Baptist,
all women of prayer.

INTRODUCTION

This is my suggestion, using your Bible:

(a) What day of the week is it?
(b) Look up the time of the day (vigil darkness of early morning, or morning, or mid day, or evening).
(c) Choose an antiphon that seems to speak to you.
(d) Read that psalm or canticle from your Bible, and choose a word or image that seems to speak to you.
(e) Write the word (or phrase or image) in this book.
(f) Breathe.
(g) Pray with the word for 10 or 20 minutes, or an hour. Be open to the reality that God may have something to say to you in it.
(h) Conclude with a prayer of simple gratitude to God.

Another Way

As a regular or occasional daily prayer book, just pray the antiphons, responsories and canticles, as presented here. Then pray *lectio divina* in *lectio continua*, perhaps using the chapter-a-day, book-by-book order on page 107.

A Third Way

For a *Seven Day Retreat* using your Bible, pray through all of the psalms, canticles and readings in a week of silence. Talk daily, or at least at the beginning and conclusion, with a spiritual director, spiritual companion, or friend in prayer.

The Best Way

The best way will be the way to/through which the Holy Spirit leads you, even if that way is very far away from this book! *Lord, how are you calling me to spend time alone with you?*

PSALTER? LECTIO?

sahl'-ter   lek'-see-oh

Psalter of Lectio is for a person I know well, who had a vague desire to pray with scripture. He had not yet seen a monastery and did not know what a spiritual director is. When he entered seminary, he discovered a language of holy and honest love in the psalms. That person is me.

An unusual episode of depression (it's my cross; what's yours?) led me where it usually does, sitting very still, sometimes for an hour, sometimes for a day or more, setting aside the priest's official four-volume prayer book, praying with a small collection of psalms. Something felt different this time. Instead of the little psalm book, I went to journal notes from a seminal 8-day retreat, and found it a helpful and healing review. It left me thinking, *What if?*

What if I began to write down the psalm phrases which the Lord was daily calling me to pray in *lectio divina* into a collection I could pray on these unusual days? Anyway, this is why I put together this ***Psalter of Lectio.*** So, a better title for this prayerbook might be ***A Psalter of YOUR Lectio***, or ***A Psalter of MY Lectio***, a collection of the sacred words, phrases, or images to which the Lord leads you (me) in our own Bible, using as an outline the times of the day that the monks pray, the monastic hours of the day.

The *Psalter* is the book of Psalms of the Hebrew Scripture. There are 150 of these songs to God. According to some, the early hermits prayed all 150 psalms each day. In his *Rule* for monks, St. Benedict called the brothers to pray the 150 psalms every seven days. The psalter that is used in the standard *Liturgy of the Hours* of the church, prayed by priests, religious, and a growing number of lay faithful, adds canticles from both the Old and New Testaments and spreads them over four weeks.

Lectio is shorthand for *Lectio Divina,* which means literally "divine (or sacred) reading." In practice, the word *lectio* usually refers to a way of praying that begins with reading or listening to a passage of scripture. When we hear *lectio* described for the first time, we can easily be confused. There are several most excellent studies of *lectio divina.* You will find on the next two pages a short description of its traditional four steps. It is as important to disregard whatever is unhelpful as it is to discover what does help.

The French Trappist Abbot Andre Louf insists on this:
Right from the beginning, prayer has already begun before I do anything… Long before I am aware of it or before I take interest in it, this prayer (of the heart) is going on ceaselessly within me. (*The Cistercian Way,* Cistercian Publications, 1983, pg. 73)

It's not so much that we pray, but that the Spirit itself prays within us with inarticulate groans (Romans 8:26). Let us listen in on that, and see what happens.

WHAT IS *LECTIO DIVINA*?

lek'-see-oh div-ee'-nuh

Perhaps best practiced in a monastery or convent, this way of praying is available to everyone. Because it is so rich, it may seem complex. Keep it simple. There are four traditional steps. Use whatever is in them that helps you to simply listen to what God, who knows you and loves you completely, wishes to say to you.
You need just two things:

A. Some time, 20 minutes to an hour?
  Don't try to find the time. Make it.
B. A passage of scripture:
  Whatever you choose is where God has led you.

1. *Lectio*

Read the passage of the word of God with prayerful attention, silently, aloud, or in a whisper. Your very act of reading is itself an act of faith that God will guide you to the word or phrase or image in the biblical text through which God desires to speak. When you feel drawn or attracted to a given word or phrase or image, **stop.**

2. *Meditatio*

Breathe. Repeat the word or phrase or image over and over as you breathe. Let it sink into your mind and heart and soul and strength. Savor the word. Ask just one question: *Why this? What do you wish to say, Lord? Why this word?* Be not worried about whether you get an answer. Stay patiently with the word as long as there is feeling, insight and understanding.

3. *Oratio*

Be not afraid to enter into a spontaneous and loving dialogue with God. Talk to God as you would talk to your closest most intimate friend. Be totally honest about what you are thinking and feeling, no matter what it is. Are any memories provoked? What do you want to say to God who loves you just the way you are? Let your response in *oratio* be expressed through praise, thanksgiving, contrition, petition, desires, decisions, resolutions, commitments, dedications… God is interested in everything that you have to say and will not judge you. You get to decide whether you will integrate this Word of God into your heart, life and work, or whether you will reject it or dismiss it as of no worth or value to you.

4. *Contemplatio*

For the remainder of the prayer time you have set aside, go back to the word, phrase or image. Breathe. Relax. Simply repeat the word, phrase or image over and over. When distracting thoughts or feelings enter your mind (they will), go back to your word. There is nothing to accomplish; just give this time to the God who loves you. Sitting in God's presence in this silence, you are making an act of faith that God is working in you in God's own time and way. When your time is up, recite the Lord's Prayer in gratitude.

This summary comes from many guides, all of whom have my deep gratitude, especially Fr. Paul Wachdorf of Mundelein Seminary, north of Chicago.

Very early on a Saturday in January of 2006 I sat in a pew in the church in Petit Goave, Haiti, trying to listen to whatever God wanted to say to me. A woman approached the altar rail and with firm reverence gave it three slaps, looking first at the statue of Mary, then at the tabernacle, and then at the nativity scene, waving her arms in the air, as if trying to get the attention of an old friend on the far side of a room. My prayer is sometimes as simple as that: *Lord, here I am! Do you see me?* It's a valid way to begin.

My favorite book on prayer is still Thomas Merton's *New Seeds of Contemplation*. Someday I will go through it and count the sentences that begin with *Contemplation is...* In the end I doubt he felt he had the thing in a box. Reading Merton left me with a surprising tug to pick up the Bible. And I don't know how to read the Bible without finding myself in prayer.

Merton is the best, but I also hold heartfelt gratitude for Jesuit Mark Thibodeaux and his four ways of praying in *Armchair Mystic* (see page 12):

1. Talking At God, which I call throwing up on God, as in upchucking all the surface stuff of the moment that I need to unload on God. It can also be less messy, as when I do not really know what to say, and so I use a ready-made prayer from the tradition.

2. Talking To God, when I am in touch with what weighs down or lifts up my heart. God already knows what it is; I sometimes have to tell it to know it, awareness by way of articulation. We can also call this spontaneous prayer or extemporaneous prayer, in a dialogue heart to heart. Many faithful Christians are very good at this. There is something more.

3. Listening To God presumes that God is always saying something to us about who God is and about who we are, a fresh and intimate way God chooses to say, "I love you." Now and then this love prods us. Praying with scripture can be the doorstep to this meditation and discernment.

4. Being With God: a gift of God we can't *make* happen. Think here of the elderly couple who have said all the words, speaking love in presence. Is this what the saints call contemplation, mystical union, or the beatific vision?

In *Too Deep For Words* (see page 11), Thelma Hall led me through a recent rediscovery of *lectio divina,* by way of three faithful steps: **(A)** Take off the sandals. **(B)** Offer an honest and still-incomplete awareness of my illusions. **(C)** Listen to Jesus praying in me.

Another Trappist monk, Michael Casey in *Sacred Reading* (see page 11), challenges me with **lectio continua**,

> *"the continuous reading of the Scriptures, carried on... day to day, omitting nothing ..., (doing) honor ... to the integrity of revelation."*

Monks practice **lectio continua** with no need to read the entire Bible. For the monk outside the monastery who wishes to pray the entire Bible, I offer on page 107 the reading order that made it possible for me to finally read the whole Catholic Bible: from the shortest to the longest book. A chapter a day takes less than 4 years, like a high school diploma or a college degree? No hurry.

A Pray-er's
Partial Bibliography

The *Bible,* available under many titles, translated into every language by countless faith traditions. My favorite is the *New American Bible,* the one adapted by the Church and used in Catholic worship every day, especially on Sundays, all over the world by American speakers of English. I am grateful for the hard work of the translators, and for the *NAB* footnotes, which I find to be a superb and concise commentary on sacred scripture. Look for the 2011 edition, *New American Bible Revised Edition* (*NABRE*).

The Rule of St. Benedict in English, Timothy Fry, O.S.B., editor (paperback, Liturgical Press, 1982, 96 pages, $2.95). ***The*** source.

Michael Casey, O.C.S.O., *Sacred Reading: The Ancient Art of Lectio Divina* (Paperback, Liguori Publications, 1996, 151 pages, $12.95). This is the most helpfully thorough explanation I have found.

Thelma Hall, R.C., *Too Deep For Words: Rediscovering Lectio Divina* (Paperback, Paulist Press, 1988, 120 pages, $8.95). I especially like how she weaves in Thomas Merton's writing, and her 50 lists of 10 scripture passages each, based on themes of the Christian life

Mark Link, S.J., *Challenge: A Daily Meditation Program Based on the Spiritual Exercises of Saint Ignatius* (Paperback, Thomas More Publishing, 1993, 391 pages, $8.95)
All of Link's 2000 series are edifying, especially *Jesus 2000* and *Bible 2000: Genesis to Revelation for Busy People.*

Andre Louf, O.C.S.O., *The Cistercian Way* (Paperback, Cistercian Studies Series # 76, Cistercian Publications, February 1984, 157 pages, $14.95). For this former parish priest and *Monday Monk*, what a gift has been this description of the Trappist way of Christian living.

Thomas Merton, *New Seeds of Contemplation* (Paperback, New Directions, 2007, 208 pages, $15.95). Used copies are everywhere. A more approachable work of Merton is *Thoughts In Solitude.* You will eventually want to read also *Seven Storey Mountain.*

Mark E. Thibodeaux, S.J., *Armchair Mystic: Easing into Contemplative Prayer* (Paperback, St. Anthony Messenger Press, 2001, 180 pages, $11.95). This was very well received in a year-long parish adult faith formation program on prayer.

Vatican II, *Dei Verbum: Dogmatic Constitution on Divine Revelation,* (Promulgated by Pope Paul VI on November 18, 1965, Paperback, Pauline Books & Media, 1965, 24 pages, $3.95) This document is printed in some Catholic Bibles and it is available in pdf format at the vatican web site wwwvatican.va.

Scripture Used In This Prayer Experiment

I have had no formal studies in the Hebrew language, and know just enough Greek to appreciate what real Bible translators do. And yet, now and again, I have a sense that none of the Bible translations in the house get at what the revealed word is trying to say, or rather, to say to *me*, in *lectio divina.* After praying for a while with a word or a phrase from a psalm, when I feel the need to dig out an interlinear or word-for-word translation, God has often surprised me.

So, since *lectio divina* is generally based on a specific word or phrase, rather than a full story or passage, these crude-stilted-awkward renderings of psalms, readings, canticles, and antiphons may give the phrase that prays. The interlinear word-for-word translations mentioned on the title page by John R. Kohlenberger III (Old Testament) and Alfred Marshall (New Testament) were used heavily but not entirely. The illustration below is Mr. Kohlenberger's Psalm 23, phrase by phrase, (read right to left):

:אֶחְסָר	לֹא	רֹעִי	יְהוָה	לְדָוִד	מִזְמוֹר (23:1)
I-shall-lack	nothing	one-being-shepherd-of-me	Yahweh	of-David	psalm
מְנֻחוֹת	מֵי	עַל־	יְרַבִּיצֵנִי	דֶּשֶׁא	בִּנְאוֹת (2)
quiet-ones	waters-of	beside	he-makes-lie-down-me	greenness	in-pastures-of
צֶדֶק	בְמַעְגְּלֵי־	יַנְחֵנִי	יְשׁוֹבֵב	נַפְשִׁי	:יְנַהֲלֵנִי (3)
righteousness	in-paths-of	he-guides-me	he-restores	soul-of-me	he-leads-me
צַלְמָוֶת	בְּגֵיא	אֵלֵךְ	כִּי־	גַּם	:שְׁמוֹ (4) לְמַעַן
deep-darkness	in-valley-of	I-walk	though	even	name-of-him for-sake-of
הֵמָּה	וּמִשְׁעַנְתֶּךָ	שִׁבְטְךָ	עִמָּדִי	אַתָּה	כִּי־ רָע אִירָא־ לֹא
they	and-staff-of-you	rod-of-you	with-me	you	for evil I-will-fear not
נֶגֶד	שֻׁלְחָן	לְפָנַי	תַּעֲרֹךְ	(5)	:יְנַחֲמֻנִי
in-presence-of	table	before-me	you-prepare		they-comfort-me
כּוֹסִי	רֹאשִׁי	בַשֶּׁמֶן	דִּשַּׁנְתָּ		צֹרְרָי
cup-of-me	head-of-me	with-the-oil	you-anoint		ones-being-enemies-of-me
יְמֵי	כָּל־	יִרְדְּפוּנִי	וָחֶסֶד	טוֹב	אַךְ (6) :רְוָיָה
days-of	all-of	they-will-follow-me	and-love	goodness	surely overflow
:יָמִים	לְאֹרֶךְ	יְהוָה	בְּבֵית־	וְשַׁבְתִּי	חַיָּי
days	for-length-of	Yahweh	in-house-of	and-I-will-dwell	lives-of-me

See Mr. Marshall's presentation of the Lord's Prayer in Matthew 6:9b-13 on page 105. I love to pray with both of them.

Any errors in the renderings offered in this book are entirely the fault and responsibility of the compiler, me, Stephen Joseph Wolf.

PSALTER COMPARISON

Psalms of the Four-Week Psalter

	Office of Readings				Morning Prayer			
	I	II	III	IV	I	II	III	IV
SUN	1	104	145	24	63	118	93	118*
	2			66	149	150	148	150*
	3							
MON	6	31	50	73	5	42	84	90
	9A				29	19A	96	135
TUE	10	37	68	102	24	43	85	101
	12				33	65	67	144
WED	18A	39	89A	103	36	77	86	108
		52			47	97	98	146
THU	18B	44	89B	44	57	80	87	143
				90	48	81	99	147A
FRI	35	38	69	55	51	51*	51*	51*
					100	147B	100*	147B*
SAT	132	136	107	50	119-19	92	119-14	92*
					117	8	117*	8*

Psalms of *Psalter of Lectio*

	VIGILS: Office of Readings	LAUDS: Morning Prayer
SUN	134/ 1, 2, 66, 104	67/ 63, 118, 148, 149, 150
MON	134/ 9, 31, 50, 73	117/ 5, 19, 29, 42, 90, 96
TUE	134/ 10, 37, 68, 102	100/ 24, 33, 43, 65, 85, 101, 144
WED	134/ 18, 39, 89, 103	95A/ 36, 47, 77, 86, 97, 98
THU	134/ 3, 6, 44, 105	95B/ 57, 48, 80, 81, 87, 99, 143
FRI	134/ 35, 38, 55, 69	117/ 51, 95, 13, 75, 94, 100, 147
SAT	134/ 4, 12, 106, 107	100/ 92, 8, 84, 93, 108, 146

PSALTER COMPARISON

Psalms of the Four-Week Psalter

	Mid Day Prayer				Evening Prayer				Night
	I	II	III	IV	I	II	III	IV	I-IV
SUN	118	23	118	23*	110	110*	110*	110*	91
		76		76*	114	115	111	112	
MON	19B	119-6	119-12	119-17	11	45	123	136	86*
	7	40	71	82	15		124		
				120					
TUE	119-1	119-7	119-13	119-18	20	49	125	137	143*
	13	53	74	88*	21		131	138	
	14	54							
WED	119-2	119-8	119-14	119-19	27	62	126	139	31
	17	55	70	94		67	127		130
			75						
THU	119-3	119-9	119-15	119-20	30	72	132	144	16
	25	56	79	128	32				
		57*	80*	129					
FRI	119-4	119-10	22	119-21	41	116A	135	145	88
	26	59		133	46	121			
	28	60		140					
SAT	119-5	119-11	119-10	119-22		119-14 113	122	141	4
	34	61	34	45	16	116B	130	142	134
		64							

Psalms of *Psalter of Lectio*

	Mid Day Prayer	VESPERS: Evening Prayer	Night
SUN	119, 23, 64, 76, 119	110, 111, 112, 114, 115, 91	4, 91
MON	119, 7, 71, 82, 120	11, 15, 45, 123, 124, 136	4, 91
TUE	119, 14, 53, 54, 74	20, 21, 49, 125, 131, 137, 138	4, 91
WED	119, 17, 28, 52, 70	27, 62, 67, 126, 127, 139	4, 91
THU	119, 25, 56, 60, 79	30, 32, 72, 128, 129, 132, 145	4, 91
FRI	119, 22, 26, 59, 133	41, 46, 88, 116, 121, 135	4, 91
SAT	119 34, 40, 61, 140	16, 113, 122, 130, 134, 141, 142	4, 91

SUNDAY — VIGILS Office of Readings

Opening Prayer
(back cover)
+ *O Lord, open my lips…*

Invitatory: Psalm 134
(back cover)

Psalm 1   Like a tree planted near streams of water.

Psalm 2   Why do the nations rage?
Blessings on all who take refuge in God.

Psalm 66   Shout to God all you earth.

Psalm 104   You breathe your Spirit, they are created,
and you renew the faces of earth.

Lectio Continua (see pages 9 and 107)

Closing Prayer   + *Let us praise the Lord,*
And give God thanks.

LAUDS **Morning Prayer** **SUNDAY** 17

Opening Prayer

+ O God, come to my assistance,
O Lord, make haste to help me.

Glory to the Father and to the Son
and to the Holy Spirit,
As it was in the beginning, is now,
and will be for ever. Amen.

Invitatory: Psalm 67

May God be gracious to us and bless us,
may God's faces shine upon us.
How else can your ways be known on the earth
and your salvation among all the nations?

May the peoples praise you, God,
may the peoples praise you, all of them.

May the nations be glad and sing for joy
for you rule the peoples
and guide nations of the earth into justice.

May peoples praise you, God,
may the peoples praise you, all of them.

The land will yield her harvest,
God will bless us,
and all the ends of the earth
will revere our God.

Glory to...   As it was...

18 SUNDAY *LAUDS* Morning Prayer

Psalm 63:2-9 My soul she thirsts for you, my God;
my body he longs for you.

Daniel 3:57-90 Let all the earth bless the Lord.

Psalm 118 Blessed is the one coming
in the name of the Lord.

Daniel 3:52-57 As did the three with one voice,
praise and glorify and bless God.

LAUDS **Morning Prayer**　　　　　　　　**SUNDAY** 19

Psalm 148　　　　　　Praise the Lord from the heavens.

Psalm 149　　　　　　Let the people of Zion
　　　　　　　　　　　　be glad in their Ruler.

Psalm 150　　　　　　Let all that has breath
　　　　　　　　　　　　praise the Lord.

---

20 **SUNDAY**   *LAUDS* Morning Prayer

Choose One Reading

1	2
Revelation 7:9-17	**Ezekiel** 36:22-28

3	4
Ezekiel 37:1-14	**2 Timothy** 2:1-13

Responsory to Reading 1 or 3:

Lord Jesus Christ, Son of the living God…

…have mercy on us.

You are seated at the right hand of the Father…

…have mercy on us.

Glory to…

Lord Jesus Christ, Son of the living God,
have mercy on us.

Responsory to Reading 2 or 4:

We give thanks to you, Lord…

…calling on your name.

We proclaim and make known your deeds…

…calling on your name.

Glory to…

We give thanks to you, Lord,
calling on your name.

LAUDS **Morning Prayer**   **SUNDAY** 21

Gospel Canticle of Zechariah   Luke 1:68-79

✝ Blessed be the Lord the God of Israel
who chose a people to visit with redemption,
and raised salvation in the house of David,
saving strength from God's own servant,

speaking from the age of the prophets
through the mouth of the holy prophet:
Salvation out of enmity,
even out of those who hate us,

to show our ancestors how mercy works, -
and to remember the holy promise of the Lord,
the covenant made for our ancestor Abraham,
calming our fear and making us free
to serve with holy justice before God all our days.

And you also child -
will be called a prophet of the Most High
for you will go before the Lord to prepare his way
and give to people a knowledge of salvation
known in accepting forgiveness of their sins.

From the tender mercy of our God,
a sun rising from the height will visit with light
for those who sit in the dark or shadow of death,
and to guide our feet into the way of peace.

Intercessions & the Lord's Prayer

Closing Prayer   *✝ May the Lord bless us,*
protect us from all evil,
and bring us to everlasting life. ***Amen.***

SUNDAY — Midday Prayer

Opening Prayer
(back cover)
+ O God, come to my assistance…

Psalm 119:1-16
(Aleph & Beth)

Blessed are ones keeping
the statutes of the Lord.

Psalm 23

My Lord lays me down
in green pastures.

Psalm 64

Let the just rejoice
and take refuge in the Lord.

Psalm 76

Giver of Light you are, more majestic
than mountains of game.

Midday Prayer   **SUNDAY** 23

Psalm 119:161-176   May your hand be a help to me
(Shin & Taw)   for your precepts I have chosen

Closing Prayer   + *Let us praise the Lord,*
                                And give God thanks.

AN EASTER PRAYER FOR VOCATIONS

Come, Holy Spirit, fill the hearts of your faithful;
set fire in us your confirming love.
Give us wisdom to seek the face of God,
understanding of our baptism in Christ,
and right judgment to discern his call in freedom.
Give us courage to say yes to our vocations,
knowledge of what Jesus teaches,
and reverence for the ways of the Abba.
Give us wonder and awe in your presence,
that the witness we give to the resurrection of the Son
may be pleasing to the Abba
and help you, Holy Spirit,
renew the face of the earth.
Amen.

SUNDAY *VESPERS* **Evening Prayer**

Opening Prayer
(back cover)
+ O God, come to my assistance…

Psalm 110 You are a priest to forever
in the order of Melchizedek.

Psalm 111 Remembered are the deeds of wonder
by the gracious and compassionate Lord.

Psalm 112 Blessed are those hungry and thirsty
for justice; they will be satisfied. (Mt 5:6)

Psalm 114 Tremble, earth,
at the presence of the Lord.

VESPERS **Evening Prayer** **SUNDAY**

Psalm 115 Not to us, Lord, not to us,
 but to your name give glory.

Revelation 19: Praise our God, all you servants of
 1b,2a,3b,5b,6b,7 the Lord, you small and you great
 who hold God in awe.

1 Peter 2: Be ready always with a word
 21-24 for everyone asking about
 (in Lent) the hope in you.   (1 Ptr 3:15b)

Psalm 91 Have no fear of terror at night;
 in the shadow of the Almighty find rest.

26 SUNDAY   *VESPERS* Evening Prayer

Choose One Reading

1	2
2 Corinthians 1:3-7	**2 Thessalonians** 2:13-17

3	4
1 Peter 1:3-12	**Hebrews** 12:18-24

Responsory to Reading 1 or 3:
May all creation sing of your ways…
…for great is your glory.
And praise the words of your mouth…
…for great is your glory.
Glory to…
May all creation sing of your ways,
for great is your glory.

Responsory to Reading 2 or 4:
Great is our Lord…
…and mighty in power.
Unlimited in understanding…
…and mighty in power.
Glory to…
Great is our Lord
and mighty in power.

VESPERS **Evening Prayer**　　　　　　　　SUNDAY 27

Gospel Canticle of Mary　　　　　　　　Luke 1:46-55

+ My soul is stretched full with praise of the Lord,
and my spirit, beyond joy in God, my Savior,
who chose to lay eyes on this humble servant.

Behold, now and forward,
each and every age will call me blessed,
for the Mighty One did great things to me.

Holy is the name and the mercy
to generations and generations,
the ones fearing the One,

Who scattered the haughty of mind and heart,
pulled the powerful off their high place,
and exalted with dignity the humble in need.

The hungering are filled with good things,
the rich are sent away empty,
and servant Israel is given relief

with a memory of mercy to remember,
the promise spoken to our ancestors,
to Abraham and his descendants forever.

Intercessions & the Lord's Prayer

Closing Prayer　　　　*+ May the Lord bless us,*
　　　　　　　　　　　　protect us from all evil,
　　　　　　　　　　　　and bring us to everlasting life.
　　　　　　　　　　　　Amen.

28 MONDAY — VIGILS Office of Readings

Opening Prayer
(back cover)

Invitatory: Psalm 134
(back cover)

+ *O Lord, open my lips...*

Psalm 9 — The Lord is a refuge for the oppressed, the stronghold in times of trouble.

Psalm 31 — Lord, shine your faces on your servant.

Psalm 50 — I desire mercy and not sacrifice, knowledge of God rather than burnt offerings. (Hosea 6:6, Mt 9:13, 12:7)

Psalm 73 — Surely, good to Israel is God to those pure of heart!

Lectio Continua (see pages 9 and 107)

Closing Prayer

+ *Let us praise the Lord,*
And give God thanks.

LAUDS **Morning Prayer** **MONDAY** 29

Opening Prayer

+ O God, come to my assistance,
O Lord, make haste to help me.

Glory to the Father, and to the Son,
and to the Holy Spirit,
As it was in the beginning, is now,
and will be for ever.   Amen.

Invitatory: Psalm 117

Praise the Lord, all you nations;
and give glory, all peoples.

Great is this steadfast love toward us,
the fidelity of the Lord to forever.

Hallelujah!

Glory to the Father, and to the Son,
and to the Holy Spirit,

As it was in the beginning, is now,
and will be for ever.   Amen.

30 MONDAY — *LAUDS* Morning Prayer

Psalm 5 Lord, hear my morning voice;
with my morning request before you, I wait.

Psalm 19 The heavens declare the glory of God.

Psalm 29 Worship the Lord in the holy splendor.

Psalm 42 When can I go and meet the faces of God?

Psalm 90 May the favor of the Lord God rest upon us
and make good the work of our hands.

LAUDS Morning Prayer — MONDAY

Psalm 96 — Sing to the Lord and praise the name.

1 Chronicles 29:10b-13 — Now, our God, we praise your name and your glory.

Sirach 36:1-5,10-13 — Show mercy, Lord, to the people called by your name.

Isaiah 2:2-5 — Come, let us go up the mountain of the Lord.

Isaiah 42:10-16 — Praise the Lord from the ends of the earth.

MONDAY — *LAUDS* Morning Prayer

Choose One Reading

1	2
2 Thessalonians 3:6-16	**Jeremiah** 15:16

3	4
James 2:1-13	**Judith** 8:25-27

Responsory to Reading 1 or 3:
Blessed be the Lord, the God of Israel…
…blessed from now and to forever.
The One alone doing marvelous deeds…
…blessed from now and to forever.
Glory to…
Blessed be the Lord, the God of Israel,
blessed from now and to forever.

Responsory to Reading 2 or 4:
How good to sing praise to our God…
…and give God the praise that is fitting.
How pleasant to sing a new song…
…and give God the praise that is fitting.
Glory to…
How good to sing praise to our God
and give God the praise that is fitting.

LAUDS Morning Prayer   MONDAY   33

Gospel Canticle of Zechariah   Luke 1:68-79

+ Blessed be the Lord the God of Israel
who chose a people to visit with redemption,
and raised salvation in the house of David,
saving strength from God's own servant,

speaking from the age of the prophets
through the mouth of the holy prophet:
Salvation out of enmity,
even out of those who hate us,

to show our ancestors how mercy works, -
and to remember the holy promise of the Lord,
the covenant made for our ancestor Abraham,
calming our fear and making us free
to serve with holy justice before God all our days.

And you also child -
will be called a prophet of the Most High
for you will go before the Lord to prepare his way
and give to people a knowledge of salvation
known in accepting forgiveness of their sins.

From the tender mercy of our God,
a sun rising from the height will visit with light
for those who sit in the dark or shadow of death,
and to guide our feet into the way of peace.

Intercessions & the Lord's Prayer

Closing Prayer   *+ May the Lord bless us,*
protect us from all evil,
and bring us to everlasting life. ***Amen.***

MONDAY   **Midday Prayer**

Opening Prayer
(back cover)
+ O God, come to my assistance…

Psalm 119:17-40   Do good to your servant;
(Gimel, Daleth & He)   I will live and obey your word.

Psalm 7   Lord, my God, save me;
                             in you I take refuge.

Psalm 71   You are my hope, Lord;
                             my confidence since my youth.

Psalm 82   One is the lawgiver and judge,   (James 4:12)
                 the one able to save and destroy;
                 who are you to be judging your neighbor?

Midday Prayer   MONDAY

Psalm 120   In my distress I call on the Lord who answers me.

Closing Prayer   + *Let us praise the Lord,*
And give God thanks.

SPIRITUAL ADOPTION in the GOSPEL OF LIFE

Living God of Israel, Christ, Son of the living God, Holy Spirit, Advocate, One God with many names, I lift up to you today one unborn child at risk, one newborn needing care, one mother afraid or confused, one father with faltering courage, one aging sage in poor health, one human alive on death row, one victim of violence or torture, one civilian in the crossfire of war, one keeper of peace in danger, one man wrestling with prejudice, one woman in need of a neighbor, one hard worker who is still poor, one migrant worker seeking dignity, one teen needing encouragement, one child having difficulty learning, one family without good health care, one community suffering pollution, and one in need of your grace. As you made each in your image, so you call us to grow into the likeness of the Risen Christ. Let each day of this year bring an advent of hope, a new nativity of faith, lenten solidarity of love, the new way of easter joy, and your abiding pentecost presence. As you have called me by name, and I am yours, so do I adopt them in prayer and beg you grant what you know they need to have life and to the full. AMEN.

MONDAY   *VESPERS* **Evening Prayer**

Opening Prayer
(back cover)
+ O God, come to my assistance...

Psalm 11   Blessed are you poor,   (Luke 6:20b)
for yours is the reign of God.

Psalm 15   Blessed are the clean of heart,
for they will see God.   (Matthew 5:8)

Psalm 45   You, my Ruler, excel among humanity,
anointed with grace on your lips.

Psalm 123   Our eyes are to the Lord
till our God shows to us mercy.

VESPERS **Evening Prayer** **MONDAY** 37

Psalm 124 Our help is in the name of the Lord,
the Maker of heavens and earth.

Psalm 136 Give thanks to the Lord,
whose faithful-loyal-steadfast
(*hesed*) love is to forever.

Ephesians 1:3-10 By God's good pleasure and purpose,
a stewardship of the fullness of time
heads up all things in Christ.

MONDAY — *VESPERS* Evening Prayer

Choose One Reading

1
Colossians 1:9-14

2
1 Thessalonians 2:13

3
James 4:1-12

4
1 Thessalonians 3:9-13

Responsory to Reading 1 or 3:
You, Lord, are the one who can heal me…
…for it is you I have grieved.
Lord, show to me your mercy…
…for it is you I have grieved.
Glory to…
You, Lord, are the one who can heal me,
for it is you I have grieved.

Responsory to Reading 2 or 4:
When I call, Lord, hear my voice…
…which rises up to you.
Like incense set before you…
…which rises up to you.
Glory to…
When I call, Lord, hear my voice,
which rises up to you.

VESPERS **Evening Prayer**   **MONDAY** 39

Gospel Canticle of Mary   Luke 1:46-55

+ My soul is stretched full with praise of the Lord,
and my spirit, beyond joy in God, my Savior,
who chose to lay eyes on this humble servant.

Behold, now and forward,
each and every age will call me blessed,
for the Mighty One did great things to me.

Holy is the name and the mercy
to generations and generations,
the ones fearing the One,

Who scattered the haughty of mind and heart,
pulled the powerful off their high place,
and exalted with dignity the humble in need.

The hungering are filled with good things,
the rich are sent away empty,
and servant Israel is given relief

with a memory of mercy to remember,
the promise spoken to our ancestors,
to Abraham and his descendants forever.

Intercessions & the Lord's Prayer

Closing Prayer   *+ May the Lord bless us,*
protect us from all evil,
and bring us to everlasting life.
Amen.

40 TUESDAY VIGILS Office of Readings

Opening Prayer
(back cover)

Invitatory: Psalm 134
(back cover)

+ *O Lord, open my lips…*

Psalm 10 You hear, Lord, the desire of the afflicted; defend the orphaned and the oppressed.

Psalm 37 Wait for the Lord and keep to the way; the meek will inherit the land.

Psalm 68 Peoples of the earth, sing to God; sing praise to the Lord.

Psalm 102 Lord, let my cry for help come to you; hide not your face from me.

Lectio Continua (see pages 9 and 107)

Closing Prayer   + *Let us praise the Lord,*
And give God thanks.

LAUDS **Morning Prayer** **TUESDAY** 41

Opening Prayer

+ O God, come to my assistance,
O Lord, make haste to help me.

Glory to the Father, and to the Son,
and to the Holy Spirit,
As it was in the beginning, is now,
and will be for ever.   Amen.

Invitatory: Psalm 100

Shout for joy to the Lord, all you earth!
Serve the Lord with gladness!
Come into the presence with joyful song.

Know that the Lord is God, who made us,
whose people we are,
in whose pasture we are the sheep.

Enter the gates with thanksgiving,
go into the courts with praise!

Give thanks and give praise to the Name!
Good is the Lord, and loving to forever,
and faithful through generations and generation.

Glory to the Father, and to the Son,
and to the Holy Spirit,

As it was in the beginning, is now,
and will be for ever.   Amen.

TUESDAY — *LAUDS* Morning Prayer

Psalm 24 The clean of hand and pure of heart ascend to the mountain of the Lord.

Psalm 33 Praise is fitting for the upright.

Psalm 43 Lord, send forth your light and your fidelity.

Psalm 65 For you, O God, praise we owe; to you will our vow be fulfilled.

Psalm 85 Lord, you show favor to your land; you forgive the iniquity of your people.

LAUDS **Morning Prayer** **TUESDAY** 43

Psalm 101 To you, Lord, I will sing praise;
I will take care to act with integrity.

Psalm 144 What, Lord, is a human that you care for us?
Children of humans that you think of them?

Tobit 13:1b-8 Blessed be God and the reign forever.

Isaiah 38:10-14,17b-20 Lord, save us all the days of our lives.

Isaiah 26: My soul yearns for you in the night;
1-4, 7-9, 12 within me my spirit longs for you.

Daniel 3:26-27,34-41 Lord, take not from us your mercy.

TUESDAY   *LAUDS* Morning Prayer

Choose One Reading

1
Romans 13:11-14

2
1 Thessalonians 5:1-11

3
1 John 4:7-21

4
Isaiah 55:1-11

Responsory to Reading 1 or 3:
In you, Lord, I take refuge…
…you, Lord, are my hope.
My trust, O Lord, from my youth,…
…you, Lord, are my hope.
Glory to…
In you, Lord, I take refuge;
you, Lord, are my hope.

Responsory to Reading 2 or 4:
Lord, hear my voice,…
…my hope is in your word and your promise.
Awake in the watch for dawn, I cry for help…
…my hope is in your word and your promise.
Glory to…
Lord, hear my voice,
my hope is in your word and your promise.

LAUDS **Morning Prayer** **TUESDAY** 45

Gospel Canticle of Zechariah   Luke 1:68-79

+ Blessed be the Lord the God of Israel
who chose a people to visit with redemption,
and raised salvation in the house of David,
saving strength from God's own servant,

speaking from the age of the prophets
through the mouth of the holy prophet:
Salvation out of enmity,
even out of those who hate us,

to show our ancestors how mercy works, -
and to remember the holy promise of the Lord,
the covenant made for our ancestor Abraham,
calming our fear and making us free
to serve with holy justice before God all our days.

And you also child -
will be called a prophet of the Most High
for you will go before the Lord to prepare his way
and give to people a knowledge of salvation
known in accepting forgiveness of their sins.

From the tender mercy of our God,
a sun rising from the height will visit with light
for those who sit in the dark or shadow of death,
and to guide our feet into the way of peace.

Intercessions & the Lord's Prayer

Closing Prayer   *+ May the Lord bless us,*
protect us from all evil,
and bring us to everlasting life. ***Amen.***

TUESDAY — Midday Prayer

Opening Prayer
(back cover)
+ O God, come to my assistance...

Psalm 119:41-64
(Waw, Zayin & Heth)

I pondered my ways
and turned my steps to your decrees.

Psalm 14

If we say we have no sin,
we deceive ourselves;
if we confess our sins,
God is faithful and forgiving.   (1 John 1:8,9)

Psalm 53

Let Jacob rejoice, let Israel be glad.

Psalm 54

See! God is helping me;
the Lord sustains my very self.

Midday Prayer   **TUESDAY**

Psalm 74   Remember, O God,
your people you gathered of old.

Closing Prayer   + *Let us praise the Lord,*
And give God thanks.

SUSCIPE

Take, Lord, and receive all my liberty,
my memory, my understanding, and my entire will,
all I have and call my own.
You have given all to me; to you, Lord I return it.
Everything is yours; do with it what you will.
Give me only your love and your grace.
That is enough for me.

St. Ignatius of Loyola

NADA TE TURBE

Nothing can trouble, nothing can frighten.
Those who seek God shall never go wanting.
Nothing can trouble, nothing can frighten.
God alone fills us.

St. Teresa of Avila

TUESDAY — VESPERS Evening Prayer

Opening Prayer
(back cover)
+ O God, come to my assistance…

Psalm 20 Now I know that the Lord saves the chosen anointed.

Psalm 21 Be exalted, Lord, in your strength; we will sing and praise your might.

Psalm 49 You cannot serve God and mammon; where your treasure is there also will your heart be. (Matt 6:24b,21)

Psalm 125 The Lord surrounds the people from now and to forever more.

VESPERS **Evening Prayer**   **TUESDAY** 49

Psalm 131   I have become still
                      and quiet in my soul.

Psalm 137:   If I forget you, Jerusalem,
1-6   may my right hand forget its skill.

Psalm 138   Before those so-called "gods"
                       I will sing my praise of You.

Revelation   Lord, out of every tribe and tongue
4:8b,11;   and people and nation,
5:9,10,12,13b   you made for our God
                       a realm of royals and priests.

TUESDAY — VESPERS Evening Prayer

Choose One Reading

1
1 John 3:1-2

2
Romans 3:21-31

3
Romans 12:1-8

4
Colossians 3:5-17

Responsory to Reading 1 or 3:

The love of the Lord endures to forever…

…for God is good.

Faithful love to all generations…

…for God is good.

Glory to…

The love of the Lord endures to forever
for God is good.

Responsory to Reading 2 or 4:

You will make known to me the path of life…

…fullness of joy in your presence.

Eternal pleasure at your right hand,…

…fullness of joy in your presence.

Glory to…

You will make known to me the path of life,
fullness of joy in your presence.

VESPERS **Evening Prayer** **TUESDAY** 51

Gospel Canticle of Mary   Luke 1:46-55

+ My soul is stretched full with praise of the Lord,
and my spirit, beyond joy in God, my Savior,
who chose to lay eyes on this humble servant.

Behold, now and forward,
each and every age will call me blessed,
for the Mighty One did great things to me.

Holy is the name and the mercy
to generations and generations,
the ones fearing the One,

Who scattered the haughty of mind and heart,
pulled the powerful off their high place,
and exalted with dignity the humble in need.

The hungering are filled with good things,
the rich are sent away empty,
and servant Israel is given relief

with a memory of mercy to remember,
the promise spoken to our ancestors,
to Abraham and his descendants forever.

Intercessions & the Lord's Prayer

Closing Prayer   *+ May the Lord bless us,*
protect us from all evil,
and bring us to everlasting life.
Amen.

WEDNESDAY — VIGILS Office of Readings

Opening Prayer
(back cover)
+ *O Lord, open my lips…*

Invitatory: Psalm 134
(back cover)

Psalm 18   I love you, Lord, my strength.

Psalm 39   What am I looking for now, Lord?
My hope she is in you.

Psalm 89   Lord, you made a covenant with your chosen and will not take back your love.

Psalm 103 My soul, praise the Lord,
whose benefits are not to be forgotten.

Lectio Continua (see pages 9 and 107)

Closing Prayer   + *Let us praise the Lord,*
And give God thanks.

Opening Prayer

+ O God, come to my assistance,
O Lord, make haste to help me.

Glory to the Father, and to the Son,
and to the Holy Spirit,
As it was in the beginning, is now,
and will be for ever.   Amen.

Invitatory: Psalm 95A

Come, let us sing to the Lord;
let us shout to our saving Rock.
Let us come before the faces with gratitude
and make a joyful noise.

The Lord is the great God,
the great Ruler above all those little "g" gods,
holding in hand the depths of earth
and peaks of mountains,
the sea and dry land formed in the hand.

Come, let us worship and bow and kneel
before the Lord who made us.
For God is our God, and we are the people
of the pasture and flock and care of our God.

Glory to the Father, and to the Son,
and to the Holy Spirit,

As it was in the beginning, is now,
and will be for ever.   Amen.

WEDNESDAY — *LAUDS* Morning Prayer

Psalm 36 Lord, in your light we see light.

Psalm 47 Sing praises to God, sing praises.

Psalm 77 God in your holiness way,
what "god" is as great as God?

Psalm 86 Bring joy to your servant,
for to you, Lord, I lift up my soul.

Psalm 97 The Lord reigns; let the earth be glad.

LAUDS **Morning Prayer**   **WEDNESDAY**

Psalm 98   Shout for joy before the Lord, the Ruler!

Judith 16:
1,13-16
O Lord, you are great and glorious,
wonderful in strength and unbeatable.

1 Samuel 2:1-10
(Hannah's Prayer)
My heart rejoices in the Lord,
humbling and exalting.

Isaiah 33:13-16   Blessed is the one working justice
and speaking honesty.

Isaiah 61:10-62:5   My God has clothed me
in garments of salvation.

56 WEDNESDAY *LAUDS* Morning Prayer

Choose One Reading

1
Tobit 4:15-19

2
Romans 8:28-39

3
Job 1:21

4
Deuteronomy 4:32-40

Responsory to Reading 1 or 3:
Push and pull my heart…
…as is your will, my Lord.
Keep my feet on your path…
…as is your will, my Lord.
Glory to…
Push and pull my heart
as is your will, my Lord.

Responsory to Reading 2 or 4:
My soul will boast in the Lord…
…and at all times.
Praise always on my lips…
…and at all times.
Glory to…
My soul will boast in the Lord,
and at all times.

LAUDS **Morning Prayer**   **WEDNESDAY** 57

Gospel Canticle of Zechariah   Luke 1:68-79

✢ Blessed be the Lord the God of Israel
who chose a people to visit with redemption,
and raised salvation in the house of David,
saving strength from God's own servant,

speaking from the age of the prophets
through the mouth of the holy prophet:
Salvation out of enmity,
even out of those who hate us,

to show our ancestors how mercy works, -
and to remember the holy promise of the Lord,
the covenant made for our ancestor Abraham,
calming our fear and making us free
to serve with holy justice before God all our days.

And you also child -
will be called a prophet of the Most High
for you will go before the Lord to prepare his way
and give to people a knowledge of salvation
known in accepting forgiveness of their sins.

From the tender mercy of our God,
a sun rising from the height will visit with light
for those who sit in the dark or shadow of death,
and to guide our feet into the way of peace.

Intercessions & the Lord's Prayer

Closing Prayer   *+ May the Lord bless us,*
protect us from all evil,
and bring us to everlasting life. ***Amen.***

WEDNESDAY — Midday Prayer

Opening Prayer
(back cover)
+ O God, come to my assistance…

Psalm 119:65-88
(Teth, Yodh & Kaph)

Teaching from your mouth is more precious than vaults full of silver and gold.

Psalm 17

Lord, hold my steps to your paths.

Psalm 28

My heart trusts in the Lord and I am helped.

Psalm 52

I trust in God's unfailing love forever and ever.

Midday Prayer   **WEDNESDAY**

Psalm 70   I am poor and needy, God;
come quickly.

Closing Prayer   + *Let us praise the Lord,*
And give God thanks.

ADVENT & CHRISTMAS PRAYER FOR VOCATIONS

Abba, you call us
to prepare the way for Christ our Lord,
bringing low the mountains of our pride
and filling up the valleys of our weakness.
As you created us in your own image,
open our minds and hearts
to know our longing for the Savior.
Help us to follow the example of Mary,
always ready to do your will.
As we celebrate the simple beauty
of the incarnation of your Son,
help us in freedom to say "yes" to our vocation
and make us radiant with his light.
We ask this through Christ our Messiah.
Amen.

WEDNESDAY   *VESPERS* Evening Prayer

Opening Prayer
(back cover)
+ O God, come to my assistance…

Psalm 27   The Lord is my light and my salvation;
whom shall I fear?

Psalm 62   My soul finds rest in God alone
from whom is my salvation.

Psalm 67   May God be gracious to us and bless us;
may God's faces shine upon us.

Psalm 126   Sowers are now in tears;
they will reap with a song of joy.

VESPERS Evening Prayer   **WEDNESDAY**

Psalm 127   Lord, build the house;
                           Lord, watch over the city.

Psalm 139   How precious to me, God,
                           are your designs,
                           how vast are they,
                           the sums of them.

Colossians 1:12-20   He is firstborn of all creation;
                           he is before all things
                           and in him
                           all things hold together.

WEDNESDAY — *VESPERS* Evening Prayer

Choose One Reading

1	2
James 1:19-27	**1 Peter 5:5b-11**

3	4
Ephesians 3:14-21	**1 John 2:1-6**

Responsory to Reading 1 or 3:
Redeem me, my Lord and my God…
…and in your grace have mercy.
Sweep me not with those doing badness…
…and in your grace have mercy.
Glory to…
Redeem me, my Lord and my God,
and in your grace have mercy.

Responsory to Reading 2 or 4:
Keep us, O Lord…
…as the apple of your eye.
Hide us in the shade of your wings…
…as the apple of your eye.
Glory to…
Keep us, O Lord, as the apple of your eye.

VESPERS **Evening Prayer**   **WEDNESDAY**

Gospel Canticle of Mary   Luke 1:46-55

+ My soul is stretched full with praise of the Lord,
and my spirit, beyond joy in God, my Savior,
who chose to lay eyes on this humble servant.

Behold, now and forward,
each and every age will call me blessed,
for the Mighty One did great things to me.

Holy is the name and the mercy
to generations and generations,
the ones fearing the One,

Who scattered the haughty of mind and heart,
pulled the powerful off their high place,
and exalted with dignity the humble in need.

The hungering are filled with good things,
the rich are sent away empty,
and servant Israel is given relief

with a memory of mercy to remember,
the promise spoken to our ancestors,
to Abraham and his descendants forever.

Intercessions & the Lord's Prayer

Closing Prayer   *+ May the Lord bless us,*
protect us from all evil,
and bring us to everlasting life.
Amen.

THURSDAY — VIGILS Office of Readings

Opening Prayer
(back cover)
+ *O Lord, open my lips...*

Invitatory: Psalm 134
(back cover)

Psalm 3 You, Lord, shield around me, my glorious One, you lift my head.

Psalm 6 Be merciful to me, Lord, and heal me.

Psalm 44 They won victory not by their sword and their arm, but by your right hand and arm and the light of your faces.

Psalm 105 Look to the Lord, to the strength; seek always the faces of the Lord.

Lectio Continua (see pages 9 and 107)

Closing Prayer + *Let us praise the Lord,*
And give God thanks.

LAUDS **Morning Prayer**   **THURSDAY**

Opening Prayer

+ O God, come to my assistance,
O Lord, make haste to help me.

Glory to the Father, and to the Son,
and to the Holy Spirit,
As it was in the beginning, is now,
and will be for ever.   Amen.

Invitatory: Psalm 95B

Come, let us worship and bow and kneel
before the Lord who made us.
For God is our God, and we are the people
of the pasture and flock and care of our God.

"If today you hear this voice
 do not harden your heart,
 as at Meribah and the desert day at Massah
 where your ancestors tested me;
 they tried me though they saw my work.

For forty years was my anger on that generation,
the people straying in their heart;
and so they did not know my ways,
and so were unable to enter my rest."

Glory to the Father, and to the Son,
and to the Holy Spirit,

As it was in the beginning, is now,
and will be for ever.   Amen.

THURSDAY — LAUDS Morning Prayer

Psalm 57 Awake, soul; wake up the harp and lyre; I will wake up the dawn.

Psalm 48 Great is the Lord, greatly being praised in the city of our God.

Psalm 80 Shepherd of Israel, awaken your might; come to our salvation.

Psalm 81 Sing for joy to God our strength.

Psalm 87 Glorious things are being said of you, city of God.

LAUDS **Morning Prayer** **THURSDAY**

Psalm 99 Exalt the Lord, our God;
and worship at the holy mountain.

Psalm 143:1-11 Bring in the morning, Lord,
your word of unfailing love.

Jeremiah 31: 10-14 My people will be filled with
my bounty, declares the Lord.

Isaiah 12 Make the deeds of the Lord
known among the nations.

Isaiah 40: 10-17 The Sovereign Lord comes with power:
with ruling arm, reward, and recompense.

Isaiah 66: 7-14a The Lord says, see! I extend peace like a river,
and wealth of nations like a flooding stream.

THURSDAY — *LAUDS* Morning Prayer

Choose One Reading

1	2
Isaiah 66:1-2	**Romans 14:13-19**

3	4
1 Peter 4:7-11	**Romans 8:14-27**

Responsory to Reading 1 or 3:
Out of the depths I cry to you...
...Lord, hear my voice!
My desire is to do your desire...
...Lord, hear my voice!
Glory to...
Out of the depths I cry to you;
Lord, hear my voice!

Responsory to Reading 2 or 4:
On my bed through the watch of night...
...O Lord, I think of you.
You who are my help...
...O Lord, I think of you.
Glory to...
On my bed through the watch of night;
O Lord, I think of you.

LAUDS **Morning Prayer** **THURSDAY**

Gospel Canticle of Zechariah Luke 1:68-79

+ Blessed be the Lord the God of Israel
who chose a people to visit with redemption,
and raised salvation in the house of David,
saving strength from God's own servant,

speaking from the age of the prophets
through the mouth of the holy prophet:
Salvation out of enmity,
even out of those who hate us,

to show our ancestors how mercy works, -
and to remember the holy promise of the Lord,
the covenant made for our ancestor Abraham,
calming our fear and making us free
to serve with holy justice before God all our days.

And you also child -
will be called a prophet of the Most High
for you will go before the Lord to prepare his way
and give to people a knowledge of salvation
known in accepting forgiveness of their sins.

From the tender mercy of our God,
a sun rising from the height will visit with light
for those who sit in the dark or shadow of death,
and to guide our feet into the way of peace.

Intercessions & the Lord's Prayer

Closing Prayer *+ May the Lord bless us,*
protect us from all evil,
and bring us to everlasting life. ***Amen.***

THURSDAY — Midday Prayer

Opening Prayer
(back cover)
+ O God, come to my assistance...

Psalm 119:89-112
(Lamedh, Mem & Nun)

I see a limit to all perfection,
but your commands, Lord,
are without boundary.

Psalm 25

Turn to me, Lord, and be gracious
for I am lonely and afflicted.

Psalm 56

In God I trust, I will not be afraid;
what can a human do to me?

Psalm 60

O God, you break our defenses;
you were angry, now restore us.

Midday Prayer   **THURSDAY** 71

Psalm 79   Help us, God of our salvation;
                            deliver us and forgive our sins
                            for the sake of your name.

Closing Prayer   + *Let us praise the Lord,*
                            And give God thanks.

ORDINARY TIME PRAYER FOR VOCATIONS

Abba, you call us to the table of your Son,
renew us by word and sacrament,
and send us to labor in your harvest.
We are a people in need of the witness
of faithful marriages and priests,
parents who know you love them,
generous single people and deacons,
religious sisters, brothers, monks and nuns.
Help each disciple to trust in your call,
make us able and willing to do what you ask,
keep us united in our gifted diversity,
and bring to maturity every seed you sow.
We ask this through the Good Shepherd:
Jesus Christ, your Son and our Lord.
Amen.

THURSDAY *VESPERS* Evening Prayer

Opening Prayer
(back cover)
+ O God, come to my assistance…

Psalm 30 Lord my God, I cried to you for help
and you healed me.

Psalm 32 Blessed is the human against whom
the Lord does not count sin,
the one forgiven of faults.

Psalm 72 I will make you a covenant of the people,
a light for the nations. (Isaiah 42:6b)

Psalm 128 May the Lord bless you from Zion;
see the prosperity of Jerusalem
all the days of your life.

VESPERS **Evening Prayer**   **THURSDAY**

Psalm 129 The Lord, the Just,
cut free the cords of bad doings.

Psalm 132 Let us go to your dwellings, Lord;
your saints will sing for joy.

Psalm 145 In every day I will praise you,
I will proclaim your great deeds.

Revelation
11:17-18; Now have come
12:10-12a the salvation and power
and reign of our God.

THURSDAY   *VESPERS*   Evening Prayer

Choose One Reading

1	2
1 Peter 1:3-9	**Colossians 1:21-29**

3	4
1 Peter 3:8-11	**1 Peter 1:22-25**

Responsory to Reading 1 or 3:
The Lord our God feeds us…
…and with finest of wheat.
Honey out rock to satisfaction…
…and with finest of wheat.
Glory to…
The Lord our God feeds us
and with finest of wheat.

                        Responsory to Reading 2 or 4:
                The Lord is my shepherd…
                  …nothing shall I lack.
                My Lord lays me down in green pastures…
                  …nothing shall I lack.
                Glory to…
                The Lord is my shepherd;
                nothing shall I lack.

VESPERS Evening Prayer   THURSDAY   75

Gospel Canticle of Mary   Luke 1:46-55

+ My soul is stretched full with praise of the Lord,
and my spirit, beyond joy in God, my Savior,
who chose to lay eyes on this humble servant.

Behold, now and forward,
each and every age will call me blessed,
for the Mighty One did great things to me.

Holy is the name and the mercy
to generations and generations,
the ones fearing the One,

Who scattered the haughty of mind and heart,
pulled the powerful off their high place,
and exalted with dignity the humble in need.

The hungering are filled with good things,
the rich are sent away empty,
and servant Israel is given relief

with a memory of mercy to remember,
the promise spoken to our ancestors,
to Abraham and his descendants forever.

Intercessions & the Lord's Prayer

Closing Prayer   *+ May the Lord bless us,*
protect us from all evil,
and bring us to everlasting life.
Amen.

76 FRIDAY — VIGILS Office of Readings

Opening Prayer
(back cover)

Invitatory: Psalm 134
+ *O Lord, open my lips...* (back cover)

Psalm 35 Awake, my God and Lord,
and rise to my defense.

Psalm 38 I confess my iniquity, forsake me not,
my Lord, my salvation.

Psalm 55 Cast your cares on the Lord,
who will sustain you.

Psalm 69 I am worn out from calling out; my throat is
parched and my eyes fail, looking for my God.

Lectio Continua (see pages 9 and 107)

Closing Prayer + *Let us praise the Lord,*
And give God thanks.

LAUDS **Morning Prayer**   **FRIDAY**

Opening Prayer

+ O God, come to my assistance,
O Lord, make haste to help me.

Glory to the Father, and to the Son,
and to the Holy Spirit,
As it was in the beginning, is now,
and will be for ever.   Amen.

Invitatory: Psalm 117

Praise the Lord, all you nations;
and give glory, all peoples.

Great is this steadfast love toward us,
the fidelity of the Lord to forever.

Hallelujah!

Glory to the Father, and to the Son,
and to the Holy Spirit,

As it was in the beginning, is now,
and will be for ever.   Amen.

FRIDAY — LAUDS Morning Prayer

Psalm 51 Lord, open my lips
and my mouth will proclaim your praise.

Psalm 95 God is our God, and we the people
of the pasture and flock
and care of our God.

Psalm 13 My heart rejoices, Lord, in your salvation.

Psalm 75 God is the one judge.

Psalm 94 The Lord knows the thoughts of humans.

LAUDS Morning Prayer — FRIDAY

Psalm 100 Come into the presence with joyful song.

Psalm 147 Glorify the Lord, Jerusalem!

Isaiah 45: 15-25
There is no god apart from me,
God just and Saving;
there is none but me.

Habakkuk 3:2-4,13a,15-19
Even in wrath
you remember mercy.

Jeremiah 14: 17-22 We are aware, Lord, of our no-good ways;
indeed we ourselves sin against you.

Tobit 13: 8-11,13-15
Children of the just,
rejoice and exult, be gathered together
and bless the Lord of the ages.

FRIDAY *LAUDS* Morning Prayer

Choose One Reading

1
Ephesians 4:25-32

2
Ephesians 2:11-22

3
2 Corinthians 12:1-10

4
Galatians 2:15-21

Responsory to Reading 1 or 3:
Bring word at break of day…
…in your unfailing love.
Show the way for me to go…
…in your unfailing love.
Glory to…
Bring word at break of day
in your unfailing love.

Responsory to Reading 2 or 4:
The Most High has kept me in favor…
…with all my heart I will keep God in mind.
May the Most High rescue me from captivity…
…with all my heart I will keep God in mind.
Glory to…
The Most High has kept me in favor;
with all my heart I will keep God in mind.

LAUDS Morning Prayer   FRIDAY 81

Gospel Canticle of Zechariah   Luke 1:68-79

+ Blessed be the Lord the God of Israel
who chose a people to visit with redemption,
and raised salvation in the house of David,
saving strength from God's own servant,

speaking from the age of the prophets
through the mouth of the holy prophet:
Salvation out of enmity,
even out of those who hate us,

to show our ancestors how mercy works, -
and to remember the holy promise of the Lord,
the covenant made for our ancestor Abraham,
calming our fear and making us free
to serve with holy justice before God all our days.

And you also child -
will be called a prophet of the Most High
for you will go before the Lord to prepare his way
and give to people a knowledge of salvation
known in accepting forgiveness of their sins.

From the tender mercy of our God,
a sun rising from the height will visit with light
for those who sit in the dark or shadow of death,
and to guide our feet into the way of peace.

Intercessions & the Lord's Prayer

Closing Prayer   *+ May the Lord bless us,*
protect us from all evil,
and bring us to everlasting life. **Amen.**

82 FRIDAY — Midday Prayer

Opening Prayer
(back cover)
+ O God, come to my assistance…

Psalm 119:113-136
(Samekh, Ayin & Pe)

Lord, I am your servant;
give me discernment.

Psalm 22

My God despised not
nor disdained nor hid from
those suffering affliction.

Psalm 26

I trust in the Lord without waver.

Psalm 59

Protect me, God,
from those who rise up against me.

Midday Prayer FRIDAY

Psalm 133   The multitude of believers
was heart and soul one.   (Acts 4:32a)

Closing Prayer   + *Let us praise the Lord,*
And give God thanks.

A LENTEN PRAYER FOR VOCATIONS

O God of compassion,
through honest awareness of sin
and the grace of repentance
you protect us from what could harm us
and lead us to what will save us.
Your Son, Jesus Christ, accepted the cross
and redeemed your sons and daughters.
Through prayer, fasting, and almsgiving
you call us each to a unique vocation
of health, healing and mercy.
May we embrace the paschal mystery and,
faithful to the gospel of Christ,
become a people who worship you
in spirit and in truth.
We ask this through Christ our Savior.
Amen.

84 FRIDAY — *VESPERS* Evening Prayer

Opening Prayer
(back cover)
+ O God, come to my assistance...

Psalm 41 Lord, have mercy on me
and heal my being.

Psalm 46 The Lord of Hosts is with us,
the God of Jacob is our fortress.

Psalm 88 I cry out day and night;
may my prayer come before you.

Psalm 116 I will lift the cup of salvation
and call on the name of the Lord.

VESPERS **Evening Prayer**   **FRIDAY**

Psalm 121   My help comes from the Lord,
Maker of heavens and earth.

Psalm 135   I know that our God is great,
greater than all the "gods."

Revelation 15: 3b-4   All the nations will come
and worship before you,
Lord God Almighty.

FRIDAY — VESPERS Evening Prayer

Choose One Reading

1
Romans 15:1-6

2
1 Corinthians 2:1-16

3
James 1:2-11

4
Romans 8:1-13

Responsory to Reading 1 or 3:

Loving us, Christ washed away our sins…
…in his own blood.
Making us a kingdom and priests to our God…
…in his own blood.
Glory to…
Loving us, Christ washed away our sins
in his own blood.

Responsory to Reading 2 or 4:
Christ died for our sins…
…while we were still sinners.
Put to death, he rose to life in the Spirit…
…while we were still sinners.
Glory to…
Christ died for our sins
while we were still sinners.

VESPERS **Evening Prayer**   **FRIDAY**

Gospel Canticle of Mary   Luke 1:46-55

+ My soul is stretched full with praise of the Lord,
and my spirit, beyond joy in God, my Savior,
who chose to lay eyes on this humble servant.

Behold, now and forward,
each and every age will call me blessed,
for the Mighty One did great things to me.

Holy is the name and the mercy
to generations and generations,
the ones fearing the One,

Who scattered the haughty of mind and heart,
pulled the powerful off their high place,
and exalted with dignity the humble in need.

The hungering are filled with good things,
the rich are sent away empty,
and servant Israel is given relief

with a memory of mercy to remember,
the promise spoken to our ancestors,
to Abraham and his descendants forever.

Intercessions & the Lord's Prayer

Closing Prayer   *+ May the Lord bless us,*
protect us from all evil,
and bring us to everlasting life.
Amen.

SATURDAY — VIGILS Office of Readings

Opening Prayer
(back cover)
+ *O Lord, open my lips…*

Invitatory: Psalm 134
(back cover)

Psalm 4   My God, be merciful to me and hear my prayer.

Psalm 12   Words of the Lord are flawless words, like silver refined in the furnace of clay.

Psalm 106   The Lord remembered for them the covenant and relented in abundant love.

Psalm 107   Give thanks to the Lord for unfailing love, for deeds of wonder for all human beings.

Lectio Continua (see pages 9 and 107)

Closing Prayer   + *Let us praise the Lord,*
And give God thanks.

LAUDS Morning Prayer SATURDAY

Opening Prayer

+ O God, come to my assistance,
O Lord, make haste to help me.

Glory to the Father, and to the Son,
and to the Holy Spirit,
As it was in the beginning, is now,
and will be for ever.   Amen.

Invitatory: Psalm 100

Shout for joy to the Lord, all you earth!
Serve the Lord with gladness!
Come into the presence with joyful song.

Know that the Lord is God, who made us,
whose people we are,
in whose pasture we are the sheep.

Enter the gates with thanksgiving,
go into the courts with praise!
Give thanks and give praise to the Name!

Good is the Lord, and loving to forever,
and faithful through generations and generation.

> *Glory to the Father, and to the Son,*
> *and to the Holy Spirit,*
>
> As it was in the beginning, is now,
> and will be for ever.   Amen.

SATURDAY — LAUDS Morning Prayer

Psalm 92 It is good to proclaim
your love in the moring
and your fidelity at night.

Psalm 8 Our Lord God, how majestic
is your name in all the earth.

Psalm 84 Blessed are the dwellers in your house,
my Ruler and my God.

Psalm 93 Mighty in the height is the Lord.

Psalm 108 My heart is steadfast, O God.

LAUDS **Morning Prayer**   **SATURDAY**

Psalm 146   I will sing praise to my God while I still am.

Exodus 15: 1-18   The Lord, my strength and my song, has become to me salvation.

Deuteronomy 32:1-12   Praise the greatness of our God.

Wisdom 9: 1-6, 9-11   Wisdom of God, come forth beside me that I may learn what pleases you.

Ezekiel 36: 22-28   I will give you a new heart and put inside you a new spirit.

92 SATURDAY — *LAUDS* Morning Prayer

Choose One Reading

1	2
Romans 12:9-21	**Philippians** 2:12-18

3	4
2 Peter 3:1-18	**2 Peter** 1:3-11

Responsory to Reading 1 or 3:
I cry to you, my Lord...
...you are my refuge.
My portion in the land of the living,...
...you are my refuge.
Glory to...
I cry to you, my Lord;
you are my refuge.

Responsory to Reading 2 or 4:
Made glad, Lord, by your deeds...
...I make music to your name.
At the works of your hands I sing for joy;...
...I make music to your name.
Glory to...
Made glad, Lord, by your deeds,
I make music to your name.

LAUDS **Morning Prayer**   **SATURDAY** 93

Gospel Canticle of Zechariah Luke 1:68-79

+ Blessed be the Lord the God of Israel
who chose a people to visit with redemption,
and raised salvation in the house of David,
saving strength from God's own servant,

speaking from the age of the prophets
through the mouth of the holy prophet:
Salvation out of enmity,
even out of those who hate us,

to show our ancestors how mercy works, -
and to remember the holy promise of the Lord,
the covenant made for our ancestor Abraham,
calming our fear and making us free
to serve with holy justice before God all our days.

And you also child -
will be called a prophet of the Most High
for you will go before the Lord to prepare his way
and give to people a knowledge of salvation
known in accepting forgiveness of their sins.

From the tender mercy of our God,
a sun rising from the height will visit with light
for those who sit in the dark or shadow of death,
and to guide our feet into the way of peace.

Intercessions & the Lord's Prayer

Closing Prayer *+ May the Lord bless us,*
protect us from all evil,
and bring us to everlasting life. ***Amen.***

94 SATURDAY — Midday Prayer

Opening Prayer
(back cover)
+ O God, come to my assistance…

Psalm 119:137-160 Your compassions, Lord, are great
(Sadhe, Qoph & Resh) as your law makes me alive.

Psalm 34 Taste and see that the Lord is good;
seek and pursue peace.

Psalm 40 My food is that I may do (John 4:34)
the will of the one who sent me.

Psalm 61 God, you are my refuge
and my tower of strength.

Midday Prayer SATURDAY 95

Psalm 140   Rescue me from humans doing bad things;
protect me from humans of violence.

Closing Prayer   *+ Let us praise the Lord,*
And give God thanks.

THE ANGELUS

The Angel of the Lord declared unto Mary
and she conceived of the Holy Spirit.   *Hail Mary…*
Behold the handmaid of the Lord;
be it done to me according to your word.   *Hail Mary…*
And the Word became flesh
and dwelt among us.   *Hail Mary…*
Pray for us, O Holy Mother of God;
that we may be worthy of the promises of Christ.

Through the message of an angel, Lord,
you made known to us the incarnation of Christ your Son;
By his passion and cross
may we share in the glory of his resurrection.
Fill us up with your grace.
Amen.

SATURDAY — VESPERS Evening Prayer

Opening Prayer
(back cover)
+ O God, come to my assistance…

Psalm 16 — In your presence will be fullness of joy, eternal pleasures at your right hand.

Psalm 113 — From the rising of the sun to its setting praised be the name of the Lord.

Psalm 122 — Pray for the peace of Jerusalem.

Psalm 130 — My soul waits for the Lord more than watchers for the morning.

VESPERS **Evening Prayer**   **SATURDAY**

Psalm 134   Praise the Lord all you servants
and ministers at night.

Psalm 141   May my prayer be lifted
as incense set before you.

Psalm 142   You are my refuge, Lord,
my portion in the land of the living.

Philippians 2:6-11   Christ Jesus humbled himself
and God highly exalted him.

SATURDAY — VESPERS Evening Prayer

Choose One Reading

1
Romans 11:30-36

2
Colossians 1:3-8

3
Hebrews 13:20-21

4
2 Peter 1:16-21

Responsory to Reading 1 or 3:
Great are the works of the Lord…
…pondered by all who delight in them.
Praise enduring for deeds of wonder…
…pondered by all who delight in them.
Glory to…
Great are the works of the Lord,
pondered by all who delight in them.

Responsory to Reading 2 or 4:
From the rising of the sun to its setting…
…praised be the name of the Lord.
The glory above the heavens,…
…praised be the name of the Lord.
Glory to…
From the rising of the sun to its setting,
praised be the name of the Lord.

VESPERS Evening Prayer   SATURDAY 99

Gospel Canticle of Mary   Luke 1:46-55

+ My soul is stretched full with praise of the Lord,
and my spirit, beyond joy in God, my Savior,
who chose to lay eyes on this humble servant.

Behold, now and forward,
each and every age will call me blessed,
for the Mighty One did great things to me.

Holy is the name and the mercy
to generations and generations,
the ones fearing the One,

Who scattered the haughty of mind and heart,
pulled the powerful off their high place,
and exalted with dignity the humble in need.

The hungering are filled with good things,
the rich are sent away empty,
and servant Israel is given relief

with a memory of mercy to remember,
the promise spoken to our ancestors,
to Abraham and his descendants forever.

Intercessions & the Lord's Prayer

Closing Prayer   *+ May the Lord bless us,*
protect us from all evil,
and bring us to everlasting life.
Amen.

AWARE PRAYER

1st MINUTE, WITH THE FATHER:

> I call to mind what has gone well this day
> and offer a prayer of gratitude.

Thanks be to you, God and Father of us all.

2nd MINUTE, WITH THE SON:

> I call to mind what has not gone well today,
> name my participation in it,
> and ask in the name of the Son for mercy.

Lord Jesus Christ, Son of the living God,
have mercy on me, a sinner.

3rd MINUTE, WITH THE HOLY SPIRIT:

> I call to mind any concerns or anxieties
> about tomorrow, next week, next month…,
> and ask the Holy Spirit for help.

Come, Holy Spirit, take hold of my life,
sign me with your holy love;
give me your gifts, confirm me in faith,
Spirit, come; Holy Spirit, help.

Mark Link, S.J., gives a most excellent take on what many call the *consciousness examen* of St. Ignatius of Loyola. My nickname for it is the *Aware Prayer,* and find it especially helpful at night. (from *Challenge 2000,* page 93; see page 11)

NIGHT PRAYER
(Sunday through Saturday)

+ O God, come to my assistance,
O Lord, make haste to help me.

Glory to the Father, and to the Son,
and to the Holy Spirit,
As it was in the beginning, is now,
and will be for ever.   Amen.

Psalm 4

When I call, answer me, saving God.
From distress you give me relief.
Be merciful to me and hear my prayer.

Until when, human, will you shame the glory?
Until when will you love delusion and seek the lie?
Know that the Lord set apart the faithful for the Lord
and will hear when I call.

When you tremble in awe, do not sin.
Search in your heart and on your bed, and be silent.
Offer sacrifices of goodness, and trust in the Lord.

Many are asking, "Who can show us good?
Lord, let the light of your faces shine upon us."

You put joy in my heart, more joy
than when their grain and new wine abound.
In the peace of God's face I will lie down and sleep,
for you alone, Lord, make me dwell in safety.

Glory to the Father and to the Son and to the Holy Spirit,
As it was in the beginning, is now, and will be for ever.

Psalm 91

One who dwells in the shelter of the Most High,
in the shadow of the Almighty, will find rest.
I will say of the Lord, my refuge, my fortress:
in my God do I trust.

Surely the Lord will save you
from fowler snare, from deadly pestilence.
With the feather of the Lord you will be covered,
and under those wings you will find refuge,
shield and rampart, the fidelity of the Lord.

You will have no fear of terror at night
nor of arrows flying by day,
of pestilence stalking in the darkness,
nor of plague that destroys at midday.

A thousand may fall at your side,
and ten thousand at your right hand;
near to you they will not come.

Observe with your eyes, simply watch;
punishment of wicked ones you will see.
Make the Lord, who is my refuge,
make the Most High your dwelling.

Harm will not befall you,
nor will disaster come near your tent. -

God's own Angels, the Lord will command
to guard you in all of your ways.

In their hands they will lift you up;
your foot will not strike against the stone.
Upon lion and cobra you will tread,
you will trample the great lion and serpent.

"Because you love me, I will rescue you,
I will protect all who know my Name.
You will call upon me and I will answer.
I am with you in trouble;
I will deliver you and honor you.

In length of days I will satisfy you,
and show you my salvation."

Glory to the Father and to the Son and to the Holy Spirit,
As it was in the beginning, is now, and will be for ever.

Reading Deuteronomy 6:4-7

Hear, Israel! The Lord our God is the one Lord!
Love the Lord, your God, with all your heart,
and with all your soul, and with all your strength.
These commands I am giving you this day
to be the commands on your heart.
Impress them on your children,
and talk about them when you sit in your house
and when you walk on the road,
when you lie down, and when you get up.

Into your hand, Lord,…   Ps 31:6
…I commend my spirit.
You have redeemed us, Lord God of truth.
…I commend my spirit.
Glory to the Father and to the Son and to the Holy Spirit;
Into your hand, Lord, I commend my spirit.

Antiphon: *   Lord, save/ us!
Save/ us while\ we are a-wake\,
pro-tect us while we are a-sleep,
that we may keep our watch/ with Christ/
and when we sleep\, rest/ in his\ peace.

Gospel Canticle of Simeon   Luke 2:29-32

+ Now, Master, you set free your servant
according to your word in peace;
my eyes have seen the salvation,
which you have prepared
before the face of all the peoples,
a light for revelation to the nations
and glory for your people, Israel.

Glory to the Father and to the Son and to the Holy Spirit,
As it was in the beginning, is now, and will be for ever.
Amen.

Repeat the antiphon.*

Our Father (Matthew 6:9b-13)

Πάτερ   ἡμῶν   ὁ   ἐν   τοῖς   οὐρανοῖς·
Father   of us   the [one] in   the   heavens:

Ἁγιασθήτω   τὸ   ὄνομά   σου·   **10** ἐλθάτω
Let it be hallowed the   name   of thee;   let it come

ἡ   βασιλεία   σου·   γενηθήτω   τὸ   θέλημά   σου,
the   kingdom   of thee; let it come about the   will   of thee,

ὡς   ἐν   οὐρανῷ   καὶ   ἐπὶ   γῆς·   **11** Τὸν
as   in   heaven   also   on   earth;   The

ἄρτον   ἡμῶν   τὸν   ἐπιούσιον   δὸς   ἡμῖν
bread   of us   -   daily   give   to us

σήμερον·   **12** καὶ   ἄφες   ἡμῖν   τὰ   ὀφειλή-
to-day;   and   forgive us   the   debts

ματα   ἡμῶν,   ὡς   καὶ   ἡμεῖς   ἀφήκαμεν
        of us,   as   indeed we   forgave

τοῖς   ὀφειλέταις   ἡμῶν·   **13** καὶ   μὴ   εἰσενέγκῃς
the   debtors   of us;   and   not   bring

ἡμᾶς   εἰς   πειρασμόν,   ἀλλὰ   ῥῦσαι   ἡμᾶς   ἀπὸ
us   into   temptation,   but   rescue   us   from

τοῦ   πονηροῦ.
 -     evil.

Hail Mary, full of grace, the Lord is with you.	Luke
Blessed are you among women,	1:28
and blessed is the fruit of your womb, Jesus.	1:42
Holy Mary, mother of God, pray for us sinners,	
now, and at the hour of our death. Amen.	

Closing Prayer   + *May the Lord grant us a restful night and a peaceful death.*
Amen.

INDEX of PSALMS

Psalm		Psalm		Psalm		Psalm		Psalm	
1	page 16	31	pg 28	61	pg 94	91	pg 25, 102	121	pg 85
2	page 16	32	pg 72	62	pg 60	92	pg 90	122	pg 96
3	pg 64	33	pg 42	63	pg 18	93	pg 90	123	pg 46
4	pg 88, 101	34	pg 94	64	pg 22	94	pg 78	124	pg 37
5	pg 30	35	pg 76	65	pg 42	95	pg 78, 53, 65	125	pg 48
6	pg 64	36	pg 54	66	pg 16	96	pg 31	126	pg 60
7	pg 34	37	pg 40	67	pg 60, 17	97	pg 54	127	pg 61
8	pg 90	38	pg 76	68	pg 40	98	pg 55	128	pg 72
9	pg 28	39	pg 52	69	pg 76	99	pg 67	129	pg 73
10	pg 40	40	pg 94	70	pg 59	100	pg 79, 41	130	pg 96
11	pg 36	41	pg 84	71	pg 34	101	pg 43	131	pg 49
12	pg 88	42	pg 30	72	pg 72	102	pg 40	132	pg 73
13	pg 78	43	pg 42	73	pg 28	103	pg 52	133	pg 83
14	pg 46	44	pg 64	74	pg 47	104	pg 16	134	pg 97
15	pg 36	45	pg 36	75	pg 78	105	pg 64	135	pg 85
16	pg 96	46	pg 84	76	pg 22	106	pg 88	136	pg 37
17	pg 58	47	pg 54	77	pg 54	107	pg 88	137	pg 49
18	pg 52	48	pg 66	78	omitted	108	pg 90	138	pg 49
19	pg 30	49	pg 48	79	pg 71	109	omitted	139	pg 61
20	pg 48	50	pg 28	80	pg 66	110	pg 24	140	pg 95
21	pg 48	51	pg 78	81	pg 66	111	pg 24	141	pg 97
22	pg 82	52	pg 58	82	pg 34	112	pg 24	142	pg 97
23	pg 22	53	pg 46	83	omitted	113	pg 96	143	pg 67
24	pg 42	54	pg 46	84	pg 90	114	pg 24	144	pg 43
25	pg 70	55	pg 76	85	pg 42	115	pg 25	145	pg 73
26	pg 82	56	pg 70	86	pg 54	116	pg 84	146	pg 91
27	pg 60	57	pg 66	87	pg 66	117	pg 29, 77	147	pg 79
28	pg 58	58	omitted	88	pg 84	118	pg 18	148	pg 19
29	pg 30	59	pg 82	89	pg 52	119	pg 22,...	149	pg 19
30	pg 72	60	pg 70	90	pg 30	120	pg 35	150	pg 19

A READING PLAN for *Lectio Continua*

from the shortest book to the longest

One Chapter a Day:
4 months shy of 4 years

13 verses - 2nd John	6 - 1 Timothy	22 - Revelation
15 vs. - 3rd John	6 - Baruch	22 - 1 Kings
21 vs. - Obediah	7 - Micah	24 - Luke
23 vs. - Philemon	8 - Song of Songs	24 - Joshua
25 vs. - Jude	9 - Amos	24 - 2 Samuel
2 Chapters - Haggai	10 - Ezra	25 - 2 Kings
3 Chptrs - 2 Peter	10 - Esther	27 - Leviticus
3 - 2 Thessalonians	12 - Ecclesiastes	28 - Matthew
3 - Titus	13 - 2 Corinthians	28 - Acts
3 - Malachi	13 - Hebrews	29 - 1 Chronicles
3 - Nahum	13 - Nehemiah	31 - 1 Samuel
3 - Habakkuk	14 - Tobit	31 - Psalms 42-72
3 - Zephaniah	14 - Daniel	31 - Proverbs
4 - Philippians	14 - Hosea	34 - Deuteronomy
4 - Colossians	14 - Zechariah	36 - Numbers
4 - 2 Timothy	15 - 2 Maccabees	36 - 2 Chronicles
4 - Ruth	16 - Mark	40 - Exodus
4 - Joel	16 - Romans	41 - Psalms 1-41
4 - Jonah	16 - 1 Corinthians	42 - Job
5 - 1 Thessalonians	16 - Judith	44 - Ps. 107-150
5 - James	16 - 1 Maccabees	48 - Ezekiel
5 - 1 Peter	17 - Psalms 73-89	50 - Genesis
5 - 1 John	17 - Psalms 90-106	51 - Sirach
5 - Lamentations	19 - Wisdom	52 - Jeremiah
6 - Galatians	21 - John	66 - Isaiah
6 - Ephesians	21 - Judges	

For other Bible reading plans, visit **www.idjc.org**.

www.ingramcontent.com/pod-product-compliance
Lightning Source LLC
Chambersburg PA
CBHW030332080526
44584CB00012B/823